happiness is …

happiness is ...

500 things to be happy about

Lisa Swerling & Ralph Lazar

CHRONICLE BOOKS

SAN FRANCISCO

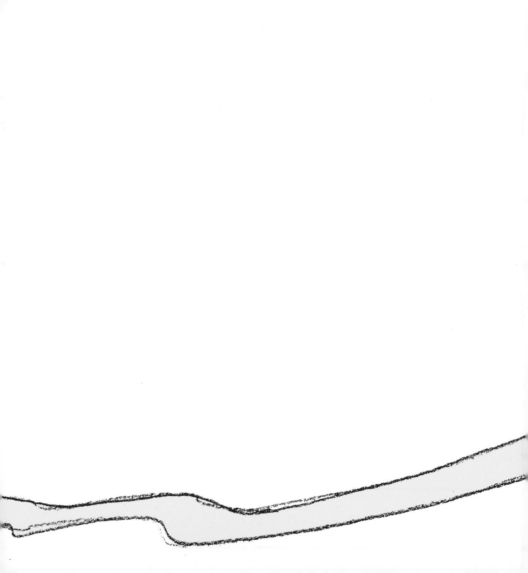

the start of a journey

a pinky promise

the chocolate bar you
forgot you had

when the vending
machine gives you extra

a view of rooftops

spooning

pottery on the wheel

extra pepperoni

when a ladybug
lands on you

a picnic

hitting a piñata

free hotel breakfast

talking music with
someone who gets it

growing a good beard

simplicity

school friends

falling asleep to the sound
of your cat purring

piggyback rides

a rocking chair

an unexpected upgrade
to business class

joining a line
just before it
gets really long

bumping into an
old teacher

a pancake
breakfast

when you're really excited to
show something to someone

tropical drinks

music that takes
you back

blowing out birthday candles

dancing like idiots

looking down on your
hometown from a plane

being the first one up

no dirty dishes in the sink

finding the perfect
pair of glasses

a freshly sharpened
pencil

spinning on an
office chair

having your work appreciated

doggy breath

saying the same thing at the same time

finding coins in the sofa

waking up to a beautiful day

chasing fireflies

when someone's laugh is
funnier than the joke

being unapologetically
yourself

fancy stinky cheese

skiing

using a pen 'til the very last drop of ink

having weird friends

a long bath with a
good book

breakfast in bed

a hug

a spoonful of
peanut butter

fixing
something

kids helping without being asked

sunrise from a surfboard

rocking out in the car with
the windows down

passing notes during lectures

laughing at a bad movie

secretly holding hands

meeting someone who loves the
same books you do

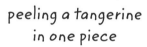

peeling a tangerine
in one piece

new guitar strings

a library

when you look fabulous
in a group photo

when someone else
catches the spider
for you

going really high on a swing

a warm cat curled up
on your lap

sugar cubes

silly mirrors

finding a lid that fits
your Tupperware

stopping to smell the flowers

a sleeping baby

teaching

maple syrup on vanilla
ice cream

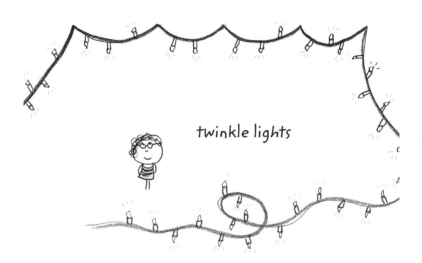

twinkle lights

making a
baby laugh

building a treehouse

making a list of all the places
you want to visit

being forgiven

a wood-burning stove

identifying constellations

finding the keys

yoga

cuddles

watching children
play make-believe

Bubble Wrap

a new language

making a wish and
believing it will come true

free mini bottles of
shampoo at a hotel

talking to your
mom when
you're sad

shopping

an adventure
with a camera

standing up for a cause

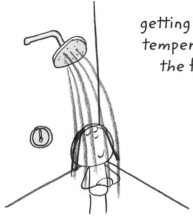

getting the shower
temperature right
the first time

a ceiling fan

a tax credit

when each sock has a pair

fresh snow and a sled

falling in love

waking up and realizing you
don't have to go in to work

twirling your hair

being annoying
on purpose

the freedom of travel

a child saying "thank you"
without being prompted

staying in on a Friday night

picking berries
on a sunny day

calling in sick

the first step

an Aha! moment

fireworks

blowing bubbles

watching a kid eat an ice-cream cone

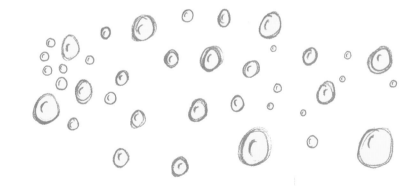

waking up next to the
love of your life

a bowl of perfectly ripe
strawberries

eating last night's pizza
for breakfast

drinking wine in good company

sewing by hand

having a best friend

pool noodles

scissors sliding through
wrapping paper

a window seat on a bus

messing around on a boat

taking goofy pictures

a front-door good-night kiss

watching waves crashing

bacon

the sight of the
pizza-delivery
guy

winning a board game

getting to the
bar just in time
for happy hour

a day spent in nature

playing with cousins

an unexpected discount
at checkout

the wind just before a
summer storm

getting lost
in a beautiful
painting

finding money in
jeans you haven't
worn in a while

seeing a cheerful umbrella

celebrating with a little bubbly

chocolate chip cookies fresh from the oven

discovering a great new song

pretending to be a mermaid
in a swimming pool

finding a power outlet at the airport

recovering data from a
dead computer

holding a baby chick

hearing your parents'
stories from back in
the day

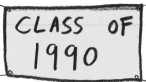

a high school reunion

sitting beneath a willow tree

rolling down all the
windows and letting
your hair fly

not having to wait in line

a duet

the cold side of
the pillow

watching a friend get married

jumping into a lake

making lists

having the elevator already
waiting on your floor

video games

buying flowers
for yourself

building a
snowman

an ambitious moustache

a photo booth

dancing tango

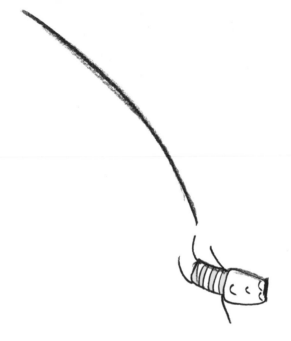

knowing that there is someone
there to catch you

autumn leaves

a fully charged cell phone

running through sprinklers

making s'mores

having a partner
in crime

a big hug from a
small person

when the dish you
ordered turns out to be
the best at the table

 being winked at by
someone nice

riding bicycles

looking forward, not back

a mother's cooking

finally peeing when you
really need to

riding in a car parallel to a fast-moving train

when your favorite sushi comes around on the conveyor belt

people-watching

a comfortable silence

remembering that word you
couldn't remember yesterday

feeling you are
heading in the
right direction

writing on a
steamy mirror

snorting while laughing

using chopsticks
correctly

getting lost in a novel

changing your own tire

cheese

an empty inbox

sunshine through the leaves

being home alone

cotton candy

going through old photos

being your own boss

feeling safe in
someone's arms

laughing so hard that milk
comes out of your nose

the sound of popcorn popping

new plants

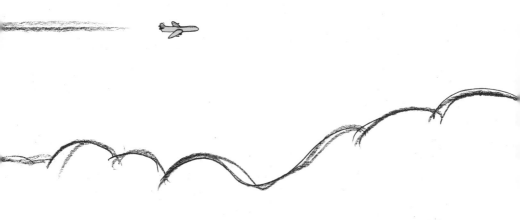

the view of clouds from a plane

finally
getting that
mosquito

sock skating around
the house

remembering something totally hilarious
in a silent situation

doing nothing all day long

a coworker who becomes a friend

reading trashy
novels without guilt

freckles

walking a dog (or two)

receiving unexpected mail

a compliment
from a stranger

housemates
becoming a family

being brave

when you feel a bite on the line

trying something new

seeing your breath
in cold air

when you love
your job

toast
popping out
perfectly
done

a long banister

erasing the
whiteboard

putting on a
wetsuit

DEPARTURES

traveling without kids

platitudes that actually
make you feel better

EVERYTHING IS GOING
TO BE OK

a sleepover

looking up at the world from
under water

hunkering down in a cozy coffee shop

when
someone
stands up
for you

napping
outdoors

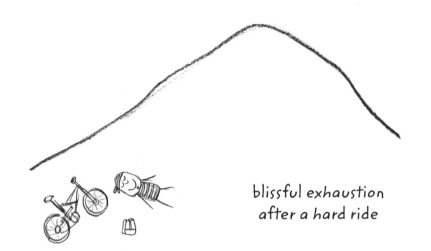

blissful exhaustion
after a hard ride

coming home to your dog

falling asleep in the room you grew up in

when your dentist says you
have perfect teeth

making it to the gas station on "E"

not taking yourself
too seriously

finding the last pair
of clean socks

when you tear a page from
a notebook and its edge is
perfectly neat

making that shot into the
wastepaper basket

crêpes!

a view of the sea

an unexpected
bouquet

remembering that you still have coffee in your cup

kids eating their food without complaint

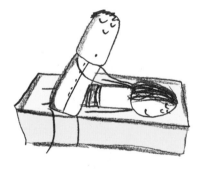

a long massage

warm clothes straight
out of the dryer

when your favorite song
comes on to the radio

knowing you're
both a little crazy

a well-dressed dog

your boss taking the day off

no homework

your favorite team winning
at the last minute

knowing where
you belong

bubblegum

first tracks on fresh snow

doing something
stupid and laughing
about it for weeks

when you're angry
with someone and they
make you laugh

beating your own record

when you suddenly
understand the
meaning of a song

bedtime stories

when the bus arrives just as you arrive

checking in at the airport
for a vacation

coming home to dinner on the table

wearing clothes that make
you feel beautiful

a good high five

handwritten letters

the view from a ski lift

leaving the car wash

laughing so hard you
pee a little

watching the
clock hit 5

eye contact
with someone
you fancy

already having all the ingredients
for a recipe

talented
street performers

rolling down a grassy hill

a fresh lemon

untamable
curly hair

finally
getting the
Hula-Hoop
going

wearing a tutu

 salty pistachios

being rescued when
you're locked out

 self-confidence

watching the trailers,
looking forward to the movie

recharging

peeling the protective sticker off a new gadget

opening a book you read on holiday and beach sand falls out

homegrown produce

balloon animals

fitting everything in
your suitcase

olives

receiving the first
birthday call just
as the clock strikes
midnight

a convertible

being together

yelling from the top
of a mountain and
hearing your echo

a night out with the girls

the perfect snowball

daydreaming

when your mom says
your hair looks nice

a water fight

decorating cupcakes

a full tank of gas

big mountains

good health

the sun on
your face on
a cold day

milk & cookies

an airport reunion

heading out on a family vacation

a fully stocked kitchen

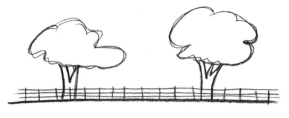

brand-new running shoes

welcoming a baby
into the world

making art

jumping in a pool
after a long, hot day

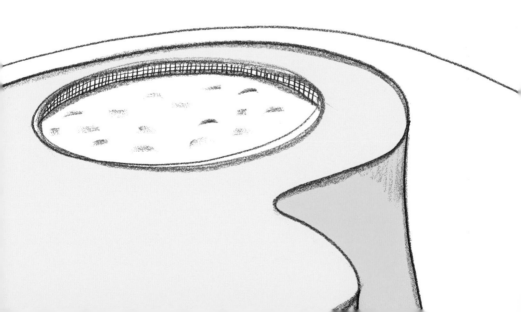

reaching the bottom of
the ironing basket

doodling

walking down an up escalator

gardening

warm bread

being swung

quality time with dad

living in your favorite city

dark chocolate

having choices

a snow globe

glitter!

a romantic date

finding the perfect
thing to wear

a serious
conversation with
a small child

the blissful
scratching of an
itchy bite

taking a road trip

kissing in the car

strong coffee

a new haircut

your first
paycheck

seeing a plant grow

wearing a hat

the smell of rain

listening to classical music

a pillow fight

crossing the finish line

margaritas on the beach

freshly washed towels

going to see your favorite band live

quitting a job you hate

a drink of cold water
after a long run

your favorite PJs

the smell of freshly cut grass

summertime

a really sharp
kitchen knife

a glass of wine in
front of the fire

overhearing the
laughter of your
loved ones

air-conditioning on a
hot summer night

being on a team

cooking with a friend

a good hair day

someone putting a blanket
over you while you sleep

getting your old password
right on the first guess

drumming

eating chips on the way back from the supermarket

sucking up a long piece of spaghetti in a single slurp

taking off your boots after a long hike

moving in together and
making a new home

dining
alfresco

finally shaving
after a few days

finding a new book by
your favorite author

speaking in a
helium voice

a buffet

texting from under
the blanket

the smell of
a baby

not taking yourself
too seriously

a yo-yo

having a pet rock

knitting

falling asleep to the sound of rain

jumping over waves

karaoke

bumping into a childhood friend

twins

a well-made bed

playing in a band

helping a
stranger

crafting things

a hot tub

sitting around a
campfire

feeling the baby kick

dancing all night

typing THE END

the sweet pain after
a hard workout

hot chocolate
with lots of
whipped cream

sunflowers

shooting hoops

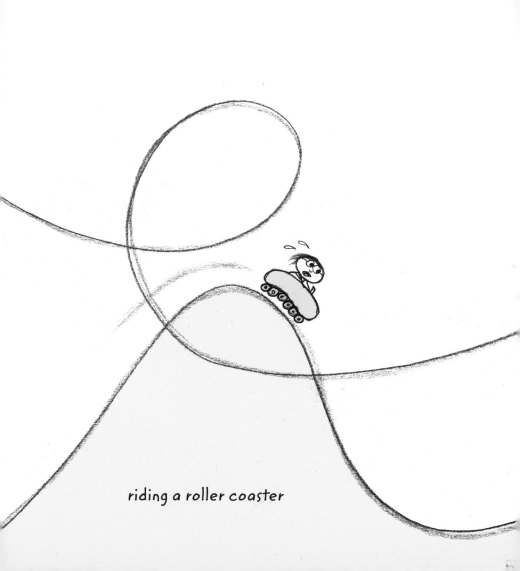

riding a roller coaster

wearing your boyfriend's
oversized T-shirt

hearing a story about
yourself as a child

watching cat videos on the Internet

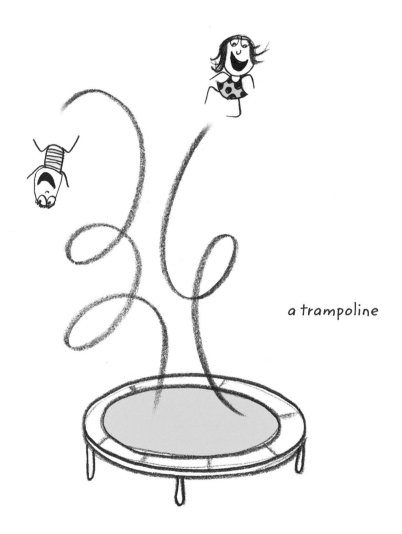

a trampoline

cozying up in a dry tent in the rain

getting rid of extra baggage

a bird landing close
without seeing you

choosing flowers in a market

the afterglow of finishing a novel

racing downhill

a butterfly

licking cake batter out of the bowl

laughing 'til your
face aches

strumming
a ukulele

the last second of
your last exam

discovering underwater worlds

venting with good friends

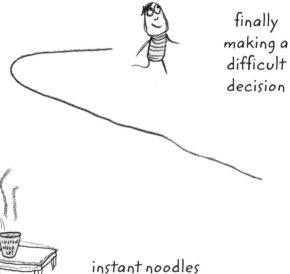

finally
making a
difficult
decision

instant noodles

kicking a soccer ball

eating anything
you want when
you're pregnant

sharing life with
your soulmate

the first page of a
new notebook

singing in a choir

a tiny garden

realizing you love your crazy family, warts and all

the smell of early-morning coffee

watching clouds change shape

cheating on your diet
and losing weight anyway

being a
traveler not
a tourist

book club

sparklers

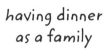

having dinner
as a family

making a giant sandwich

fresh bagels and cream cheese

the mere existence
of the didgeridoo

a nice big yawn

making others' lives easier

chatting with grandma

a bubble bath in
candlelight

the smell of freshly
washed hair

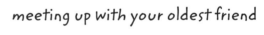

meeting up with your oldest friend

a slinky

uninterrupted TV

the smell of basil

finding that perfect shell

writing when
the words
really flow

finding a piece of
candy in a bag you
thought was empty

noticing it's
11:11 and
making a wish

booking a
vacation

watching snowflakes

a special pen

pickles

unpacking the last box

an early-morning walk

the fantasy of getting away from it all

a neat desk

a sneaky weekend break

WORK
DAILY GRIND
OFFICE
RESPONSIBILITY
BUSY BUSY BUSY

BEACH
RELAXATION
CHILL OUT ZONE
OTHER NICE STUFF

watching your man
cook dinner

a hot drink on a cold day

a slice of lime in a
cold bottled beer

sleeping diagonally

a great conversation with a stranger

wearing flowers
in your hair

reminiscing

BEACH

biking to the beach

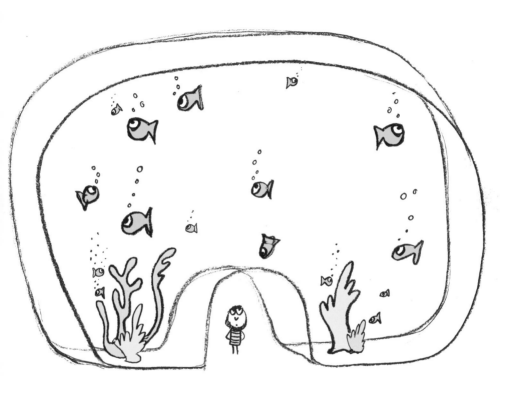

an aquarium

a long walk with a friend

setting up your own business

hot sauce

grandchildren

receiving what you ordered online

jumping in puddles

resting after a long, hard trek

untangling the
last knot

when a baby holds your
finger and refuses to let go

steak

liking
yourself

returning to bed
after a long day

playing in the warm summer rain

sleeping under the stars

leaving work on Friday

being the only one laughing ...
and not being able to stop

scaring the living
daylights out of someone

wearing new shoes
for the first time

buying yourself
something nice,
just because

being really
silly together

a costume party where everyone
makes a huge effort

parenthood

pajama parties

getting your dream job

finding the perfect pair of jeans

being engaged

finishing the crossword

a shooting star

riding a bike downhill

a head massage

getting that pesky
piece of food with a
toothpick

dropping your phone and
catching it mid-air

having a dishwasher

perfectly painted toes

sisterhood

free Wi-Fi

finding your size in
the sale items

leaving and never looking back

seeing a stranger smile while
he's reading a book

finishing a
to-do list

giving a kid a Band-Aid
for a tiny cut

receiving a love
letter

sharing an umbrella

taking off ice skates

roasting marshmallows

a fresh baguette

balloons

 the first glimpse of home after a long time away

Library of Congress Cataloging-in-Publication Data available.

ISBN 978-1-4521-3600-4

Manufactured in China

Design by Anne Kenady

10 9 8 7 6 5 4 3 2 1

Chronicle Books LLC
680 Second Street
San Francisco, CA 94107
www.chroniclebooks.com